Until The

Comes

By

Peter D Hehir

P. D. ~~Hehir~~

PETER D HEHIR

2020

ISBN: 978-1-291-63797-7

PublishNation. London
www.publishnation.co.uk

Contents

With Love

Beauty has designed you in such fabulous awe,
Like the moment an artist takes a pencil to draw.

You are Picasso's model, a statue delight
To rival the stars for the best of the night.
You are the study of Freud, desire so deep,
You can dance through the dreams where the angels
sleep.
You are Shakespeare's muse – the reason to rhyme
And the face that launches the ships of our time.
You are the thoughts of Plato, beauty and wise
Held in the magic of your sparkling eyes.
You are the symphony of Mozart, sweet to the ear,
Your smile is the music to the death of a tear.
You are the kisses of Juliet on Romeo's skin,
You are the place that I end and the place I begin.

Beauty has designed you in such fabulous awe,
Like the moment an artist takes a pencil to draw.

Why? Why? Why?

Like Samson said to Delilah
"Where have ye put me sword?"
"I'm not gonna tell ya, you beastly man
Now leave me alone!" She roared.

But this made Samson angry
As he thumped against the door,
And Delilah stood shaking behind it
As he kicked it more and more.

Then Crash! The door flung open
And Delilah hit the ground,
As Samson circled around her
With that angry thumping sound.

But then for a second he turned his back
As Delilah ran for the door,
And with blood on her knife she shouted "Forgive me –
I just couldn't take anymore!"

A Colourful Crime

The police searched through this lowly town
Paying a visit to *Mr Red*,
Then they turned their enquiries to *Mr Yellow*
And arrested him instead.

With curtains twitching at a frantic rate,
Mr Purples were drawn right back
And on Tuesday night across the way
Moving house was ol' *Miss Black*.

Then Wednesday *Mr Brown* was taken
And *Mr Green* was questioned too,
No-one was above the law
Not even *Mrs Blue!*

By daytime *Mr Pink* was watched,
With *Miss Orange* watched by night,
But who on earth on Rainbow Street
Had killed poor *Mr White*?

Doors to Manual

Turn the doors to manual
To stop them coming through,
There's thoughts in there that grey the hair
Of the younger ones we knew.

Turn the televisions off
And watch the local news,
That's limping like a broken bike
In someone else's shoes.

Turn the clocks to face the wall,
Close your eyes – rewind,
And shut the doors on all the wars
That plague your troubled mind.

Then turn to face the starry night
That leaves the day in pain,
Then smile wide at morning tide
When it all begins again.

Mr Mayfly

Just one single day to do what I choose,
Nothing to be blamed for and nothing to lose.
I could glide over water or sail on leaves
Or dance through the places where the sunlight weaves.
I could fall in love with a flower or two,
Never knowing if they feel the way that I do.
I could watch how the creatures will spend their day,
Surviving to bask in a moonlit play.
Then I'll spy on some roses that welcome the sun
Into their hearts where the rain shall run.
Down through the trees and onto the ground,
Making a splash but never a sound.
I'll live like a king; yes that's what I'll be,
Setting the colours of this picture free.
Just one single day from the moment I wake,
Twenty four hours of memories to make.

Christmas in the Graveyard

'Twas Christmas in the Graveyard
Behind the iron gates,
The calendar had shook the snow
Off all forgotten dates.

The shrines of bones were etched upon
With memories and names,
The flowers we brought were tinsel thoughts
For empty picture frames.

Their roof was made of silver stars
And their Christmas trees would sway,
Beside the soiled stony paths
Where only life would play.

Their mistletoe was holly leaves
That spread and spoilt the view,
Just covering those pale faces
Heading straight for you.

'Twas Christmas in the graveyard
Of winds that never blew...

Llamedos

Let's drop litter, let's eat meat
Evict the neighbours from our street.
Buy a shotgun, phone the police
Never iron a single crease.
Steal whatever, start a fight
Play your music late at night.
Start a gang to bust this town,
Graffiti walls then knock 'em down.
Nick a cash point – serve your time,
Any city – any crime.
Let's buy drugs and pass 'em on
To see Bob Marley on a swan.
Forge a name, rob a bank,
Someone on e-bay selling a tank.
Buy it off them, start a war,
Ask us what we're fighting for.
Call up leaders – need advice,
They tell a lie then tell it twice.
Get some gossip, pass it round,
Then pull the pin and hear the sound.

Seventeen

Memories soaked in lipstick,
Pressed against that handkerchief
Of such simple design.

Her hand on his asking, demanding
For eyes to be stared into,
Brown like an autumn of promise
That sulked back into a wintry shell.
Snakebite frost leapt with discontent
Envy at the warmth they shared.
She pursed her lips around a frozen cigarette
As he struck a match and leaned towards her,
His breath grazing against her rouge skin
In the cool night air.

The smoke rippled across his hands
To the solitude of a single flame
That teased a thousand moths,
And then died in a fabulous explosion of black.

Ophelia

Time shifts to the breaking of untouched time,
Festered to root like a crown for the poor
And rags to the king to fit with allure,
Not in such a life, or life within lime?
Who can but whisper, and hope to hear truth?
When voices tell scenes that eyes never saw
And books fall open where pages are tore,
Undying marks tell of undying proof.
But life runs right through here cold to the bone,
Lost to be found in the losing of sight,
Blinded by that of the blackest of light,
When wealthy of heart no man dies alone.

But on close of eyes she lies in defeat,
Tragically playing her symphony sweet.

Entity

What is life? But a hole in the paper,
That will deepen with the sins of the few,
The edges of this distance will taper
And the darkness will roll back into you.
Lined by a sadness on twisted escape
Until your breath is a mist in the air.
Hope is the sound of unwinding the tape
And the future of a past shall be there.
But frayed be the edges, still be your sword
As you're followed by those shadows of black,
Let fingers play to a heavens accord,
When you're just another card from the pack.

An end shall meet the beginnings we know,
It is time that stays, it is we that go.

Double Decker Dreamers

On the top deck of the bus tonight
There's music in my ears,
I look out on the passers-by
As each one disappears.

Into the darkest night of all
Outside this window pane,
Just steaming up with every breath
I write my crooked name.

But you can never read it,
For it's written in reverse,
On the top deck of the bus tonight
And the rain is getting worse.

Innocence

Eight little fingers and ten little toes,
Those swimming pool eyes and a cute button nose.
A smile of roses and the cry of a dove,
The heart of a soldier in a bundle of love.
The joy of a giggle from the tiniest sound,
The touch of a snowflake just kissing the ground.
A time to be treasured, like a seed to the rose,
With eight little fingers and ten little toes.

Rock on Nimbus Stratus

They had a fancy dress ball in heaven last night
And everyone was there,
Elvis came dressed as Robert the Bruce
And he danced with Fred Astaire.
Ghandi came posing as Elgar
But Beethoven wasn't amused,
He had heard from good vibrations that
His costume was already used.
By Henry no less of Tudor House
As he entered in Plato's robe,
Then he caught the eye of Mr Van Gogh
And his sidekick Juan Earlobe.
Then Oliver Cromwell waltzed right in,
In his best Bob Marley gear
And he said when asked about sandwiches:
"Have ya got some with Jammin dear?"
"No" Replied Kipling, keeping his head
As he circled around the room,
Then he bumped into Churchill pretending to be
Nostradamus – the profit of doom.
"I predict in the future" he went onto say
"We will fight on the beaches again"
As Nelson strolled in dressed up as King George
Screaming drunk "The Dragon is slain!"
Everyone ignored him as Einstein stood up
In a costume of Shakespeare himself,
And he shouted "Thou art merry gentlemen
Let's raise a glass to the health..."

But his words were cut short as a fight broke out
When the Tudor wives started to grapple,
As Newton sat talking down into his drink –
"I'm sure I taste hint of an apple."
Then the lights went out on every star
And clouds turned to powdery white,
But Elvis is still in the building somewhere
And we've got karaoke tonight.

Beneath the Flake

Imagine if I'd dreamt you,
I'd never want to wake,
Your hand like pebbles in my palm
With ripples left to make.

Imagine if I'd kissed you
But only as you slept,
I'd never see those smiling eyes
And all the thoughts you kept.

Imagine if I'd touched you
But never felt your touch,
It would be like I'd missed everything;
I'd feel it twice as much.

But imagine if I'd dreamt you
I'd never want to wake,
If just to feel your skin on mine
Like ground beneath the flake.

That Strawberry Curve

He'd leave his smile at the garden gate
And frown upon the path,
Where many a weed has wondered
In a rain lashed puddled bath.

He'd watch the black coal crackling
And smoke the night's cigars,
He'd shoot for the moon and miss sometimes
But still be among the stars.

The world would tire his eyes to sleep
But his dreams were just as sad,
Because the tears that he was crying
Were the best he'd ever had.

He'd murder ideas and go on the run –
A Poet trapped on the page,
And when his thoughts had gone he'd say
"The budgies flew out of the cage"

But no more breaths shall pass between
That Strawberry Curve of Red,
"Of what did he die?" they asked of me
"Oh he died of living" I said

Jar of Hearts

It's on the shelf by the picture frame,
Nearest the broken clock,
It's clearly marked but without a name
Like a barge in an empty lock.

It beats itself 'till cracks appear
And blood red stains the oak,
And there's nothing but the fear of fear
That wears a romance cloak.

There are broken smiles of enemies
And all trapped up inside,
With those many truthful memories
That just vanished when you lied.

Then it shatters where the loser wins
In a million tiny parts,
Just screaming like those violins
In my lonely Jar of Hearts.

The Great Boat Race

Your face is like a picture
That time forgot to paint,
The colours are demanding,
The pencil lines are feint.

The palette is a carnival
Of sinews spilling pain,
The canvass bursts with monochrome
And eyes of liquid rain.

Then a smile turns illusions
Into pockets full of hate,
And it all explodes with emptiness
In a story you narrate.

With expressions drawn from memory
On a landscape of regret,
Your face is looking lived in
But the sign still says 'To Let'

The Magpie and the Woodpecker

As the Magpie said to the Woodpecker
"Can you keep the noise down mate?
I'm trying to get some sleep in here
And it's getting rather late"

But the Woodpecker did not take kind
To the orders from a thief,
And he carried on peck, pecking away
To the Magpies disbelief.

So when the stars rolled back the covers
The magpie took his chance,
And stole everything the Woodpecker had
As he lay in a sleepy trance.

Then morning came as it said it would
And the Woodpecker woke to find,
That as he dreamt beneath the moon
The night had robbed him blind.

But before anyone could be accused
It was an unhappy justice he found,
As he saw the Magpie dying below
On the unforgiving ground.

So the moral of this story is;
Don't steal from your foes,
Because you'll just come back as field mice
And they'll come back as crows.

RoC

The eyebrow lift and pinned back ears
As every wrinkle disappears,
But then old age picks up its pen
And draws them all back in again.

Dandelion

Dance with me.
Like a dandelion that blows
Its timeless energy into the air.
Scattered on some far flung breeze,
Nameless to all but nature.
Colliding whispers fuse to the last
Known wonder of the gaze.
I watch and live a moment I've never seen,
Then I wonder…

Will you dance with me?

Black Valentine

A bullet for my Valentine
An arrow for her lover,
A shot then a ping
From the pull of a string,
Oh where will I find me another?

Telegram to Heaven

Standing on the edge of life with no-one else about,
Dreams and nightmares run my mind and scream to be
let out.
But time stands on my shoulders; I've nowhere else to
go,
Just close my eyes and fade away, to curtain call the
show.

My memories are mysteries, washed away to sea,
Riding waves then drowning and reflecting back to me.
I imagined my stay here timeless; to die from the day I
was born,
My soul now trapped in a fool's paradise; my heart
became heavy and worn.

Now a devils servant lost am I, but not among the few,
A wise man said "if you want change, the change must
be in you"
So here I am now at your call, I've played my final hand,
And I'm standing on the edge of life, just sinking in the
sand.

Until the Rain Comes

I will hold your hand forever 'till the rain comes
And hold you even more when it arrives,
We'll be dancing through the sunshine 'till the rain comes,
With it soaking through the fabric of our lives.

We won't be making footprints 'till the snow comes,
Just walking through the memories we made,
Then shivering and smiling when the snow comes
Drifting past the places where we played.

We will keep on chasing shadows 'till the storm comes
And I'll shelter you from harm when it appears,
I will keep you wrapped up warm until the storm comes
And use my eyes to wipe away your tears.

And we'll be looking out until the rain comes
With droplets on the windows of our lives,
I will hold your hand forever 'till the rain comes
And hold you even more when it arrives.

An Ode to Lewis Carroll
(In reply to Jabberwocky)

Beneath the sundial in the wabe
The tove began to eat,
As swiftly moved the Bandersnatch
To a fast galumphing beat.

The tulgey sky was threatening
As the clouds began to gyre,
So hid the desperate Jubjub bird
With flamed perpetual fire.

Then mimsy as it burbled
The Borogrove appeared,
The rath outgrabe and chortled
As brillig ever neared.

Then frumious and frabjous
The sun burst through the sky,
So manxome it did gimble in
The leaves that floated by;

When silence fell so quickly
And the slithy tove did flee,
As the Borogrove came whispering
Beneath the Tumtum tree.

He warned me with an uffish tone
"Beware the next attack,
For somewhere in the tulgey wood
The Jabberwock is back"

Kaleidoscope

It's a purple paradise kind of life,
Grabbing hold of love like a thrower to the knife.
It's a dripping dawn of damson in distress,
Flowing in surrender and looking more or less
Like a red mist of ribbons left untied,
Wrapped around a rainbow just as colourful and wide
As a parachute of poppies on parade,
Fading in their beauty to a monochrome cascade.
Then falling like fever to a scarlet intent,
Drowning in pools of a mandarin scent.
Just grabbing hold of love like a thrower to the knife,
It's a purple paradise kind of life.

Chalk lines

I couldn't help but notice
That smile on your face,
When you took away a part of me
That no one could replace.

You missed out all the kisses
On everything you wrote,
Where once I saw a love letter
There was a simple note.

Your lips retreated readily
When faced with my advance,
You waltzed on past my questions
And asked the world to dance.

Then I fell into chalk lines
That you began to trace,
When you took away a part of me
That no one could replace.

The One that Never Was!

It just hangs on the glass, teasing.
Covering every angle it sees
Yet not moving.
Small in exterior
But clever enough to escape.
It waits, yet so do you,
Being lured into making the first move.
Flinching. Then Stops.
You both in parallel fashion.
This process repeated until you are tested to the edge.
Temptation overcomes reality.
Yesterday's newspaper rolled slowly;
Never a sound.
Producing a cylinder shape,
Lofted up high, the moment is right,
Then smack!
What a fool you've been,
Decisive windows,
Damn fly.

Artificial Love

The stem is made out of plastic
And the petals are made from card,
For love is not that easy
And hate is not that hard.

Lovers End

Breaking heart display
Was full but yesterday,
Leaking all the love it kept
In the pockets of today.

For the Missing

The moon salutes the parachutes
Falling from the sky,
Peppering the baking earth
Where unknown soldiers lie.

Anon

He thought she loved him
Then he found; she loved him not –
She loved the pound.
He then compared true love to water,
But in an endless drought he caught her
Drinking from another's heart
Oh where to end, oh where to start.
Alas! She drowned, adieu the pound
And broke they died apart.

The Fluffy Malteser

Jesus lived in caravan,
With stained glass windows and a broken fan
And a picture of the invisible man
Just hanging on the wall.
There was nothing but bread and fish in the freezer,
Down the back of the sofa a fluffy malteser,
Left by the guy that called Jesus a geezer
And the last greatest hippie of all.

He went to Damascus pub most nights
Arrows, peanuts and drunken fights,
Then he staggered back up the lane of lights
That led him safely home.
His sandals were worn down through and through,
Through many a black and into the blue,
But he never once did as the romans do
When walking the streets of Rome.

His followers laughed at all his jokes,
And the tales of love his knowledge evokes
Of confessions on which our memory smokes,
Until it burnt his mind.
Then he got a job on the rag and bone,
While calling for people to give him a loan
Of their time to help the seeds be sewn
And their eyes to help the blind.

He had a heart of gold and a silver tongue
A big brass soul and an iron lung,
All gifts from three men wise and young,
That lived across the field.
He'd look at the stars and drink his gin,
Then lie back and watch the day begin,
To wipe with its light the blackest of sin
The night time had concealed.

But then came eviction through rent arrears,
As everyone cried recycled tears,
Over all them miracles and oh so nears
He had built his name upon.
Now some years later empty it stands,
Peppered graffiti stained window plans,
The case is now closed and out of our hands
And the fluffy malteser has gone.

Going Home

There are crowds in all the bus stops
And jokers on the stairs,
There are beggars in the doorways
And papers on the chairs.

There's trees all lined up waiting
For the summer to arrive,
Where leaves are simply falling
Just hoping to survive.

There's litter on the pavements
And puddles in the gutters,
To splash the tired buildings
With lights behind the shutters.

There are flowers on the lampposts
With stars two hours old,
There are stories in this moonlight
That the daytime never told.

On Leaving

Breaking heart?
Oh mine will start
On when we part in sorrow.
Pale moon,
You orange balloon
I'll see you soon,
Tomorrow.

On Time

Timeless whispers circle round
As the shadows melt below,
Stars like cats eyes in the night
Fall soft like flakes of snow.

And through the darkness, splinter light
Through the wrinkles of the sky,
Plants nectar bleeds upon the earth
Where weeping willows lie.

On Love

I distinguished the stars when you left
And stencilled the pale blue moon,
But it just fell apart in my fingers,
Like May fell apart into June.

Abandoned Umbrellas

Abandoned umbrellas lie drowning in puddles,
With people in bus stops in neat little huddles,
Hoping for duvets and hot chocolate cuddles
On this finest autumn day.

With Golden brown leaves that stick to the shoes
And pavements that cracked in the summertime blues,
There are triangle warnings all over the news
As the rain comes out to play.

Gardens are bouncing with hayfever kisses,
It seems to long for those wintertime wishes
And lightning strikes where another one misses,
In a place not far away.

Then the droplets all gather on the window pain,
Through an avenue just off memory lane,
And the buses are late because of the rain
On this finest autumn day.

Floodgate Street

Through the arteries of the city
And the rippling river rea,
Where history smells of old canals
And the ghosts of yesterday.

With memories full of emptiness
Their shadows tease the moon,
Wearing smiles that stretch for miles
But tears come too soon.

They wonder past the viaducts,
So lifeless to the core,
The rise and falls of factory walls
Have seen them all before.

And the stories on these cobbled streets
Will never go away,
Where the history smells of old canals
And the ghosts of yesterday.

A Little Nation

Misty magic memories making morning mist,

many men are mourning the many men we missed.

Leaping like those leopards that leap across the lye,

living like those lions that love to live a lie.

Then pouncing past this picture

those people paying praise,

a person playing purposely –

a preacher purely prays.

But singing songs of sadness

'till someone surely stares,

when someone's spirits searching

for solace on the stairs.

Then feeling fingers fidgeting,

familiar furtive feet

that famously forget to flinch –

a fine forgotten feat.

And as the magic memories move

to make the morning mist,

those many men still mourn the minds

of the many men we missed.

Pigeon Park

Benches full of businessmen and empty beer cans
There are pockets full of energy in a generations hands.

Where tombstones are the floorboards beneath forgotten
feet
And pigeons perch upon the church to gaze upon the
street.

There are bodies on the carpet green just soaking up the
sun,
Where tattoos fade in a masquerade of nothing to be
done.

And here there living side by side, from breaking dawn
'till dark
The creatures walk through daily talk in crowded pigeon
park.

Trouble in the Basement

"Foolish or stupid?"
Said the Devil to Cupid,
"I see what's inside"
Is what Cupid replied.

"I've stole heavens keys"
The Devil did tease,
"So see what's inside"
An Angel replied.

"But where is the lock?"
Said the Devil in shock,
"You're welcome inside"
The Angel replied.

"Yet how can this be
With the Devil in me?"
"For I see what's inside"
Is what Cupid replied.

The Peaky Blinders

There are whispers in the Garrison,
Now someone's stole the guns
And no one meets in the cobbled streets
That a peaky blinder runs.

We will take care of the loved ones
That we've met along the way,
But those memories and those enemies
Will die another day.

And we'll win on every gamble
Whether fighting fit or lame,
Then quell the noise of the Kimber boys
'Till the country knows our name.

Then when they know who not to cross
We'll leave the war behind,
And parlé here without a fear
When I use my peaky blind.

Shadows

There are shadows on the ceiling
But I'm sitting in the dark,
The swings are moving gently
But there's no one in the park

There's music in cathedrals
But no one's giving praise,
There's laughter in the theatres
Where no one ever plays.

There are clocks that stopped some time ago
But time moved on the same,
There's benches looking out to sea
Without a single name.

And there's dogs that howl to sunrise
But no one hears a bark,
There are shadows on my ceiling
But I'm sitting in the dark.

Slán, a ghrá
(Goodbye, my love)

When the birds greet the morning with songs of the air
I look up to the sky and I know that you're there.

When the flowers yawn widely and reach to the sun
I'll think of the good times and the things that we've
done.

Then when I see snowflakes that tickle my skin
I will finish the memories that we tried to begin,

And when I feel raindrops that splash without care
I'll look up to the sky and I'll know that you're there.

Windmill Lane

It's a hanging basket paradise
Down in Windmill Lane,
There's empty tins and wheelie bins
With a double barrelled name.

There are golden ticket chocolate wrappers
Scared to touch the ground,
They play the skies like butterflies
But never make a sound.

The street lights never flicker here
And neither do their eyes,
There are fingertips on upper lips
Where an empty rumour dies.

Then the moon sinks into puddles
And the footsteps do the same,
To fill the hole in a broken soul
Down in Windmill Lane.

The Circus Is Open

It all came to pass on the 24th day,
A man was found drunken in charge of his sleigh.
When questioned at length and asked for a name,
He said "I don't own one and Rudolph's the same;

He's resting at home with a stomach complaint,
I've only popped out for a red tin of paint!"
The police looked confused and questioned him why?
"To touch up his nose" Was his mumbled reply.

They had all they needed and read him his rights,
As his beard reflected the flashing blue lights.
He kicked and he shouted "I need to be free,
On a million old rooftops I'm destined to be"

They couldn't stop laughing on the way to the station
Not believing his stories about saving the nation.
They locked him away and filed their report:
'A man with no name who was drunken when caught,

With a red and white suit more wholly than God
And an old rusty sleigh like an Alien pod.
He failed the breath test on sherry it seemed,
He possessed more presents than a kid could have
dreamed,

Yet they must have been stolen, though he tried to
protest,
He shouted "I'm Santa!" like we couldn't have guessed,
But a pretty poor fake one just like all the others –
24th of December – signed PC Carruthers.'

The very next morning he stood in the dock,
Scratching his beard and watching the clock,
Some green elves attended and cases were made
And a sentence was passed with a fee to be paid.

He was given two months and placed in a cell,
As inmates whispered "How the mighty have fell".
The evening drew quickly he thought all was lost
But then there were footprints on the settling frost.

They were of a fairy, whom he'd helped long ago,
He showed her the way when addicted to snow,
She waited for hours and did all she could,
Until two sets of footprints came back through the mud.

She got him home safely; he slept for a while,
The joy in my heart was as big as his smile,
For the fairy paid bail and phoned me to say –
"Christmas postponed 'till the 26th day"

3am

There's an empty bottle of Chardonnay
And a lonely old cigar,
Just longing to be held again
As I wonder where you are.

The lights on in the dining room
And the door is on the latch,
There are loads of falling stars tonight
That I simply couldn't catch.

The fireplace keeps crackling
As I crawl on up the stairs,
Just thinking of those many thoughts
That no one ever shares.

Then the street lights flicker hourly
As I curl beneath the covers,
I wrote this one for me and you
And all the lonely lovers.

Duvet Days

Ben and Jerry's, duvet days,
Yawning mornings, getaways.
Heated pillows, warmer sheets,
Summer thoughts, winter tweets.
Snooze alarms, broken clocks,
Sleepy eyes, missing socks.
Stubbed toes, wet shoes,
Today's events; tomorrow's news.
White teeth, locked doors,
Footsteps, pigeon wars.
Crowded buses, work piles,
True time, false smiles.
Coffee breaks, tea stains,
Rain kissed window panes.
Home time, sore feet,
New message; funny tweet.
Boiler broke, cold shower,
TV guide, every hour.
Bed calls, dreams fade,
Nights fly, beds made.
Sunrise, replays,
Ben and Jerry's, duvet days.

Sleeping Seasons

When I'm walking through the autumn leaves
I know I'll see your face,
And I'll gather up those memories
To fill that empty space.

As flakes fall fast in wintertime
I know I'll feel your touch,
And smile as I'm shivering
To miss you just as much.

Then in the springtime serenade
I'll watch the April showers,
To hear you in the gentle breeze
And smell you in the flowers.

Then summertime; I'll stop and think
How seasons never stay,
Like you they leave those memories
That will never go away.

Letters from a Clown

Dear whoever, I write with a smile,
You should just try it if once in a while.
I juggle with fire and honk on a horn,
Where sadness is dying a smile is born.
I can also do magic and make things appear,
Like a coin from the back of a little boys ear.
I can dance through the laughter beneath the trapeze,
And watch as the faces all twinkle and tease.
I will conjure up shadows to play in the light
As handkerchiefs fold and the colours delight.
So come to the Circus and stay for a while;
*Yours and forever- **the Clown with a smile.***

Under the Midnight Sun

Stars bleeding on the cities below.
Emerald with envy
They spill mandarin liquid from their crystal casings.
The sky falls apart.
Tearing like a velvet cloth,
Fraying at every edge leaving an afterglow of amber
That kisses the darkest corners of the earth.
Blue metallic tears drop from the ledges of heaven
Into seas and into hearts.
The sapphire ceiling vibrates with a sliver pulse
That hints of flame red and golden markings
To scar the sky forever.
And as you hang the stars out to die
They drown in their platinum wounds
Under the midnight sun.

At Dawn

On the pillow where you lay before
There is a lipstick stain,
As I fold over the bed sheets
All crumpled up in pain.

There's the coldest cup of coffee
And a lonely pizza slice,
Just bitten by the night before
And swallowed by it twice.

The air just smells of passion
And that unfamiliar scent
Of the perfume on your pale skin
And the kisses that I spent.

I wash my face with memories
That the sunrise never saw,
Then dry it with the dressing gown
That you wore the night before.

Then I dress myself with tiredness
And button up my coat,
I search the empty room again
For the DVD remote.

But the mirror says *I Love You*
When the steam has gone away,
And I'm just left with lipstick stains
On the pillow where you lay.

New Year's Eve on Facebook

It was New Year's Eve on Facebook
And statuses were made,
With cocktails of fireworks
And a Vodka lemonade.
There were disaronno dreamers
And smiles made of stars,
As all those who have left us
Just smoke the night's cigars.
There were memories and enemies
We've made along the way,
Some will see another year
And some another day.
We've had festivals of laughter,
Kaleidoscopes of tears,
Overwhelming moments;
And overcoming fears.
There are jokes and poor punch lines,
We've never heard before,
We have opened every window
And knocked on every door.
So raise your glasses higher
And welcome in with glee,
A year that will be bouncing
Like a stone across the sea.

It was New Year's Day on Facebook
With Resolutions made,
And revolutions plenty;
I forgot the lemonade.